THE TOMB OF THE UNKNOWN ARTIST

Also by Andy Kissane:

Poetry
Facing the Moon (1993)
Every Night They Dance (2000)
Out to Lunch (2009)
Radiance (2014)

Fiction
Under the Same Sun (2000)
The Swarm (2012)

As Editor
Feeding the Ghost 1: Criticism on Contemporary Australian Poetry
(2018, with David Musgrave and Carolyn Rickett)
The Intimacy of Strangers (2018, with Philip Porter)

The Tomb of
the Unknown Artist

Andy Kissane

PUNCHER & WATTMANN

First published in 2019

Published by Puncher and Wattmann
PO Box 279
Waratah NSW 2298
http://www.puncherandwattmann.com
puncherandwattmann@bigpond.com

National Library of Australia
Cataloguing-in-Publication entry:

Kissane, Andy
The Tomb of the Unknown Artist

ISBN 9781925780376
1.Title
A821.3

Cover design by Tim Langford
Typeset by Christine Bruderlin
Text in Abode Garamond 12/15 pt
Printed by Lightning Source International

This project has been assisted by the Australian Government through the Australia Council, its arts funding and advisory body.

Australian Government | Australia Council for the Arts

Contents

One

Two

Three

Four

In memory of my parents
Miriam McIntyre
and Frank Kissane

One

all night
I watched him breathe.

Sharon Olds, *The Race*

Alone Again

Walking alone, my toes sinking into the wet sand
of this primordial beach, the sloshing pull
at my ankles reminding me of the dark certainty
of the womb that I can now only imagine

—that second when I slipped suddenly
into the hands of another and bawled my first
barbaric yawp into the warm pulse of the night—
a moment as precious and as easily forgotten

as the multitudes that follow. Each day begins
with snatches of birdsong, the smallest flicker
of eyelashes, a tempting laziness and a yearning
that I struggle to name and understand. While

eating alone, like a dog, in stately Vienna
and sipping what the waiter calls the best beer
in the world, I listen to Louis Armstrong sing
of the saints, the saints, and as the sax blows

heaven ever closer, I tear the sweet lamb
from the bone, the light blazing off the silver
and for once I don't think that I have wasted
my life. Hopefully, I will feel this way again

at the hour of my death, when my feet
turn blue, when a flying ant buzzes, trapped
between the blind and the window, when
I am about to fall or rise into who knows

what mysterious space, aware that I alone
can do this, and must, aware that I cannot
defer or control what will be—my eyes
now opening for one last glimpse of beauty.

The Last Quarter

Ten points down at three-quarter time
and anything is possible. You fish
a brown paper bag out of your overcoat pocket
and hold it out for me. I reach for the apple
that is mine. When I bite into the crisp flesh
you say, "We need the first goal of the last quarter."
The intimacy that only barrackers share.
The joy of watching the lanky left-footer
storm through the centre square and let fly
from a long way out, the Sherrin sailing
straight over the goal umpire's head.

Visiting you in the nursing home, I want
to reclaim those Saturday afternoons,
but there's the arctic tremor in your hands,
your old bones that don't make enough
red blood cells, that only kick behinds,
the way you doze in the green armchair
even when we're winning. Somewhere
in my own marrow lies the moment
when you fathered me, that unacknowledged
gift—the siren finally sounding,
a horde of jubilant arms lifting, elation
sweeping through the crowded terraces.

Waiting Beside You

All I can do is sit by your bed and watch you die.
I don't yet know that what I am feeding you
will become your last meal on this earth.

Spoon after spoon of thickened water
because it's easier to swallow and a few spoonfuls
of pumpkin soup, though spoon*ful* is a misnomer.

Your appetite has shrunk along with your body.
Parched lips, eyes firmly shut, your white hair combed
back against the pillow. I watch your mouth slowly opening

as I balance the spoon and tip the clear wobbling
liquid onto your tongue. Occasionally I miss and mop
your cheek with a tissue. You say, "Please"

and "Thank you" as if you have decided to teach
by example, impart the perfect manners that rarely
graced a table crowded with five boys who learnt

to eat quickly or go hungry. When I think of the word *mother*
I see you with an apron on, peeling potatoes, the black pot
simmering on the stove. I think how we took for granted

the steaming plates you placed in front of us, night after night,
how the kitchen was a no-man's-land you patrolled,
how peace was the sound of boys with heads down,

eating heartily. Everything has changed. Now we
can cook: goat curry, fish wrapped in banana leaves,
upside-down plum cake. Recipes are for sharing.

I lift the spoon to your lips and you say, "Thanks,
I've had enough." I listen to the rattle in your chest,
how each breath you take seems to fill up the room.

When I think of love I will always see a tablecloth—
knives, forks and spoons in their places, serviettes.
I will always hear your welcome cry, "Dinner is ready."

A Personal History of Joy

"… and once more saw the stars."
—Dante Alighieri

It hangs for a moment before your face—
a dandelion puff, a sheaf of smoke, wonder
before its vanishing, your exhaled breath hovering
above floodlit shadows, the lapping oval
which in winter, after heavy rain, resembles
the viscous crema on top of an espresso,
its aroma lifting, bitterness lingering on your tongue,
the caffeine hit like the exhilarating shock of an idea
that comes to you anywhere, at any time—
while digging in the vegetable patch, say,
feeling for the familiar globular solidity of a potato—
Otway Reds, glorious Dutch Creams, the pink blotches
of a King Edward that you've renamed "Goughs",
after Edward Gough Whitlam who believed in free
university education and the cultivation of all people,
no matter how much of a spud they appeared to be.

I love how we live in sensual, sensing bodies,
how when I spy the pied cormorant lurking
on the mangrove flat, then hear the flapping of wings
and look back to see that the bird has gone, I still
have a nanosecond of its presence in my head,
along with all kinds of ephemera: how as a teenager
I would dress up in my mother's stockings
because they were as close as I could get
to the scent of a woman; how diving under waves

I hear the endless rhapsody of the sea; how
walking in an angophora forest I can believe that trees
pass on their wisdom in ways we are just beginning
to understand. Recently, while roasting chicken thighs
with Jerusalem artichokes and banana shallots,
I discovered the miracle of the marinade—drowning
the pieces in a baste of olive oil, tarragon, thyme,
crushed pink peppercorns and saffron threads,
then tossing everything together until my hands
were stained yellow, the bowl a fragrant, rustic promise.

I suspect that the unmarinated life is not worth
living, that the neural pathways need to be lit
by all kinds of sources—the glow of a desk lamp
illuminating an open book, the sudden flashing
of fireflies intent on attracting a mate, the vivid streamers
of a city street captured by time-lapse photography.
In *River*, the grieving detective is visited by manifests
who talk of the lives they once shared,
just as I glimpse my father sitting on the verandah
sipping a beer, or raising the lid of the barbecue
as the swirling smoke weaves around his outstretched arm.
If you are lucky there's a twist in the tale and everything
coheres, is graced with a meaning that never seemed
possible, so when you're swung in the tackle
and thrown face-down into the mud, you lift
your head in time to see the ball spinning end over end
right over the man dressed in a white butcher's coat,
and even though thirty-five years have passed,

you can still remember how he glances in your direction
and greets your clumsy snap with a two-thumbed salute,
a perfect accompaniment to the endorphin light that swamps
your mind as you rise again into the shining world.

These Scraps

You wake after sleeping well. Before you
the ripe promise of morning. You taste
the sudden bitterness of coffee on your tongue,
think of your Ottolenghi friends who photograph
the steaming plates before eating. The boobook owl
sits pensively after a night of hunting; the bluetongue
basks on the rock ledge below the staked tomatoes.
You have just discovered a writer who makes you gasp
with pleasure. You are fifty-six and still crazy
about women—this desire that is both ache and longing.
Today is Wednesday. Another crop of habaneros
is coming on; firecrackers green and potent
before the turn. You can almost hold
these scraps of happiness in your fingers.

Walking the Murrumbidgee

Ah peace—the man in the yellow shirt
          and floppy blue hat has finally
                    taken his whipper snipper and departed
          and sunshine beckons.

          You rest your hand
on the wooden balustrade of the verandah
          as the heat seeps into your palm
                    and the scent of cut grass rises.

You despise those lazy poets
          who glimpse a cat slinking past—
                    and immediately, a curled tail, attitude
                              and a golden stare appear upon the page.

The man in the workshop asks
                    if it's really a poem and not cut-up prose
and you think, "Where were you
                    during the twentieth century?"

though you do not say this. The mind flows
                    like a river, you read somewhere,
          though walking beside this river,
the simile seems inadequate, colonial even.

You are listening to a story on your iPod
                    as you pass the stretch where a platypus
          has been sighted, a story in which time
                    rushes on and a man who drinks

a helluva lot cannot remember if his last
orgasm was any good, or even if he had one.
         You recently said "Fuck trees" to a poetry class
in an attempt to impress, to persuade them

         of the coolness of an art
that seems increasingly irrelevant in a vamped-up
               world. Ironically, you now pause
to stare at a red gum, noticing how each branch

has a working-class beauty, how the pockmarked
         peeling bark is so individual,
defying the unending replicas
               of the production line.

You check your watch to see if it's time
         for the five o'clock wave to roll past Wagga beach,
the flow released from Burrinjuck and Blowering
         building and building—until a jet ski tows

a lanky goofy-footer onto the lip of the rushing torrent
               and he swings his dreadlocks into the glassy face
                  and grins, confident of riding this baby
         all the way to Narrandera. You stroll on, wondering

why you have your wallet, scared
         that someone will jump you on the secluded path
that runs beside the billabong. But this is the Bidgee,
         not some city river, and as if to reinforce this, two ducks

slide past your face, swooping down
to what the Wiradjuri call, "plenty water".
              At times the surface
is an Impressionist painting of indistinct trees

and swatches of blue, shimmering with light.
       You love the clarity of a moving stream,
              the surprise of a dangling, swinging rope,
                     the hollering moment before you let go

and plummet into the shocking
              chill of water that was once ice
and now offers a buoyant promise—a drifting
       tractor tube with room enough for two.

A friend told you recently
       how he was in demand after his wife died—
              young, healthy, with a car and a secure job,
and how he realised that single and married men

float in completely different currents. Rivers
       are so embedded in our consciousness
that we no longer see how we are their offspring—
       how we begin underground, then bubble up

in heath and bog country, how we join
       with other streams and gather momentum
              and how at any moment of our lives
we are a droplet, a transparent surface and a deluge.

Marriage Material

When I imagined walking down the aisle
I did not know that it would feel like this:
as if I'd been blessed with much more

than I deserved, more than I could grasp: as if
this scent of gardenias and orchids would cling
to my skin for the rest of my days; as if my smile

had been fixed on my face by a changing wind;
and the battering rain a sure sign that some wants
must be endured until they pass. I am about to marry

Henry Thomas Braddock, even though he took
his own good time to propose. I'll never forget how
he hid his shaking hands in his trouser pockets,

as if he believed he was Mr Collins and I a haughty
Elizabeth Bennet about to send him on his way
like some charcoal burner with no fortune, no future

and only the banks of the Cooks River to call home.
He seemed almost shocked that I didn't want to think on it,
and startled when I suggested that because my father had

eloped with my mother, he was certain to give his blessing
to a man of independent means who proclaimed love
and respect for his daughter. "Call me Margaret,"

I advised, because that's what my father named me—
and make sure it's the last time it crosses your lips.
I am Ruby, your Ruby, and there's something in your

greeting that makes my skin tingle, my stomach
lurch. I doubt that many brides wish for rain
on their wedding day, but this raucous hammering

is sublime music to anyone who survived
the Federation drought. My father glances up
as if he'd rather be outside in his garden, digging

beetroots and filling his barrow with squash.
While the organist plays the last notes of *Ave Maria*,
the pounding rises to a crescendo then dies away.

I stand next to you in your black coat, thinking
how lucky I am to have a husband who can sew.
No darning, no pricked fingers for me. I stand there

as Dr Roseby says, "Let us rejoice, dearly beloved."
I am already rejoicing, my hand in yours, my life
laid out before me like a roll of brocade silk.

There's still the pattern to cut, the lining, the hem
to stitch, the hooks and the eyelets, but I am wearing it,
I will be wearing it all day, this surprising bliss

that is longer than my train, that fits me—just so—
and I don't understand how I know this, but I do—
this joy will be mine for as long as I live.

Dressed

This absurd lyric—all about girls and fun—
plays in your head as you drive. You want
to do this. You like the way your pencil skirt
just covers the top of your stockings, how
the sleeve of your blouse billows. A nice
contrast. Even your car is red, you think,
as you slink into an empty space.
Outside, as you pull on your ankle-length coat,
you feel the cold air on your bare thighs
and you wobble, precariously, in your heels.
You are doing what you've always wanted to do,
though you can't help glancing over your shoulder
to check who is around, who might see you.
You know how this breaks up families, you've done
the research. Inside the pub, the boys all turn
to look and you smile and let your coat fall
slightly open. You order a strawberry daiquiri.
Susan, Andrea and Louise are at their usual table.
You're Lisa tonight and the name feels delicious
as you say it. You promised you wouldn't overthink this.
Desire is pure, as clear as water, and shame—
well, you just don't feel any.

Seeing You Again

Driving to your place, I remember
how you said you wanted to carry
my hands around inside your bra.

You won't say that today. You are married
and it's years since that dinner dance,
foxtrotting under the tablecloth, my cock

wet before I'd eaten the entree.
You said you adored men in dinner suits
and I was eager to strip, loosening

the onyx studs from my ruffle slowly
and carefully, as if they were amulets
with the power to peel back my shirt,

open up my skin. You meet me
in the driveway, comfortable in tracksuit
and windcheater. Your hair is not quite

the way I remember it. We don't have
much time alone. Your husband's making
coffee in the kitchen as words ripen

on the roof of my mouth like blackberries—
fat and ready to fall. My cup wobbles
on its saucer as I recall our last camping trip,

lilos pushed together, your sleeping bag
zipped into mine, the guttural snores
of lion seals floating up from the beach.

I think of what might have been, waking
to a thousand, thousand dawns, children,
the closeness where you don't need to speak.

Instead, there's this afternoon tea, polite
conversation, the way I look at you
and wish I could live more than one life.

Courage

You would hide behind my legs
in the chicken run,
wary of their sharp beaks,
their flurry, strut and waddle,
how they flocked and flapped and brushed up
against you, as if you were the source
of all the scraps they so urgently desired.
You would not go in there without me.
Wise, to be scared of them.
Then one day, my girl, my daughter,
you pranced into the house
with a feather stuck in your hair,
your small hands wrapped around
        a warm egg,
your face beaming as if to say—
see, see, how I am holding courage
in my hands and lifting it up
for you to grasp and savour.
I remember this when I miss you,
when the war presses in on me
like a hundred mad hens,
when I feel like fleeing north
and can only stop myself,
by raising cupped hands
to my lips, as if I still have
that speckled, fragile egg
        you gave me.

Domestic Dreaming

1

It's hard not to see the idea of a house built
over a stream as romantic, especially when the channel
runs beneath the kitchen, so you can casually drop
a baited line through the hole in the floor and wait
for a bite while you have an afternoon nap.
A simple matter to scale and gut the fish, dip it
in milk and breadcrumbs and fry it in a little oil.
There is something calming about flowing water—
the liminal wash of waves on sand, the possessive
pull of a tidal river, as if deep down
we're still in touch with the amniotic certainty
of the womb, how we once floated in brine,
as content as the last anchovy left in the jar.

2

Sitting on the balcony in the late afternoon,
you hear what sounds like the crackle
of burning wood, surmise the welcoming
aroma of smoke, though you cannot see the fire
which is incinerating waste from a building site
two doors down, nor be sure that the scent
is not something you have imagined to accompany
the trilling of lorikeets, the steady drone of traffic.
You sense the radiant heat of gleaming coals,
glimpse the flames as they leap, tumble and cart-
wheel towards your outstretched palms
and realise that you don't have a mind of winter
or any desire to get one, preferring how grackle

and twizzle takes you from offcuts smouldering
in a steel drum to a flock of geese flying low
over the undulating meadows of the sea
as scattered white petals shift with the swell.

3

Consider the shoe rack at the bottom of the wardrobe,
the doll-sized flap between rooms that once held a telephone,
the tall African pot by the doorway that stores umbrellas—
these accoutrements seem as familiar and as strange
as my mind. I've heard of the lobe, cortex
and cerebellum and although they clock on daily,
I'm yet to observe their labour or comprehend
how they grow and change. I might as well be aboard
an ocean liner floundering in tumultuous waters,
grateful the captain's up there, somewhere,
on the bridge, that the radar is functioning
and a course has been plotted through the icebergs
that involves minimal risk, that leaves me free to gaze
at the stars wandering through an inky, historical sky.

4

As for the bedroom—you sleep every night
in its loose embrace. On one wall, the Modigliani nude
is still dozing in the artist's studio, an ode to beauty
playing on an endless loop, while Diego Rivera
rests in the cliff of Frida Kahlo's thick eyebrows,
as if he is always on her mind, the white threads
of her Tehuana headdress spooling out like myriad

dreamlines, while above the chest of drawers
a woman rides a Chagall rooster and a bride floats
with the sort of ecstatic freedom that you'd hope
might bless all marriages, all becomings, all voyages
into an unknown future. A giant candle flares
above a hill town, the impasto of blemished skin
shines like the crystals embedded in the chert
and quartz stones you stole from the shingle beach
near Mystery Bay. Some mornings when you wake
and lie there, as lazy as a sunning lizard, you pick
up the pebbles from the bedside table and listen
to how they scrape together in your hand,
as if they are being swept and carried
end over end by the great oceans of the world.

Two

One man will always be left
alive to tell the story.

Hannah Arendt, *Eichmann in Jerusalem*

Glen Hansard Plays the House

"Tell the people that you saw me passing through."
—Dick Blakeslee

By the time he was halfway through the opening song
he was already flying. I was not the only one to think this.
His body rode the flurries and thermals, gliding

and swooping over the bitumen-black streets
with such apparent effortlessness, such astonishing grace
that his band simply coasted along in the upwash

of his outspread wings. Even geese are not this beautiful,
I thought, and then, this is no honking hyperbole,
this is Glen Hansard strumming his guitar

with such ferocious ferocity that there's a crater
in the soundboard where his fingers have worn away
the soft cedar. Stroking his abundant beard,

he told us how The Frames were so stoked
to play the Opera House that they all took selfies
in front of the gleaming sails to send to their mothers.

When the lights went up three hours later, we trailed
out—only to see Glen and his friends busking
the forecourt for anyone who wanted more craic.

I'd have dropped a gold coin into his guitar case,
if he had one. He played on as if the pavement was his home
and the random stars in the sky had gathered to listen.

Waiting

At the appointed hour the houses migrate,
walking on their pincer legs with the surety
of a crane, taking up different allotments
in the same street. We wake to an aria
spilling from a neighbour's window, thrumming bees
who cannot find their nest, their queen.
A man's barnacled voice counts off the names
of the ships in the bay below, while the scent
of coffee wanders down the cobbled alleyways,
drifts under umbrellas and plays hide and seek
with the vanishing shade. Later, we might hire
a rowboat, oars slipping under the glassy surface
of the sea. I will scale and gut the fish we catch
while you build a small fire in the stern, so we can
reinvent the notion of freshness. Eating
the black skin will remind me of the fruit bat
who snoozes all day in the jacaranda tree,
then makes whoopee at night, crying out in a language
that lurks beyond sense. Apprehension comes slowly—
it's physical—like the heart beating in the chest,
the body aware of its own diseased state, the bluetongue
basking on the sandstone with one eye open.
So much of living involves learning how to wait,
without knowing what we are waiting for.
The blossom sticks to the wet bitumen, appearing
theatrical in the rain. We leave the darkened
cinema with our senses stretched, footsteps echoing
insistently behind us, the headlights of a Volkswagen
trailing our car as we head for home. We're hoping

that when we round the corner and slide into the driveway,
no tectonic plates have shifted in our absence, that
our house is still where we left it three hours earlier.

Getting away with it

It started as a joke.
I couldn't write anything, so I
stole a few short lines

from Robert Creeley,
then drove real fast
without considering the desti-

nation.
Soon Bashō's frog was leaping
out of a woodblock

& into my notebook, although
I wasn't stupid enough to toss
Elizabeth's fish back into the sea.

Before I could cite the cento defence,
I'd won the Blake, the Newcastle
& the Ethel Malley urn. Now

the truth is out, I'm crawling
through the stink
of a sewer, struggling

to breathe.
The bottom rungs of the ladder
are impossibly high,

while a sniper waits
near the manhole to blow
my head off.

I dress in my shame every day—
a suit of beautiful words
I long to call my own.

Riding the Rotor with No End in Sight

You can't even make time
to kick a football with your own son,
my wife says one night,
when my boy is already asleep.
I drop him at Before School Care
each morning & tell him
to have a good day. Work's busy
at the moment, I say.
I want to tell him that I love him,
but I don't. I manage change in others,
not myself. I just work.

I work smarter, harder, longer.
The wall behind me spins
& my non-iron business shirt clings
to it. My laptop & mobile phone
stick as well. The floor slips away,
yet I don't fall. I'm safe up here.
Sex is merely a memory
I'm too tired to have.
This is *my* life, I might think,
if there was time to think.

But there are calls to take,
meetings to arrange, work
to do. My stomach churns.
I'm stranded. I want to wake
into another tomorrow
where I'm not pressed up
against this spinning wall,
where I can defy more than gravity,
where choices are mine to make
and my son's wobbling punt
falls into my waiting arms.

Modern Whaling

This is no Quaker graveyard in Nantucket,
where, at least, the sperm whale had half
a chance—thrashing her flukes
against the sloop's wooded hull,
or diving below the harpoon's deadly reach.
This is the productive artistry of modern whaling
which strives for best practice, the way
the Japanese Captain takes out the cow first
so the bull will surface beside her, howling
for the love of his monogamous life,
a sitting target of blubber and barnacles,
huge beside the ice floes of early spring.
Soon to be nothing but a culinary delicacy
and a lament—sung with a hand held over a heart,
sung so the whale's last breath rhymes with death.
Is this the measure of our progress—gelignite
stealth flensing the sky to a rainbow white?

Thunderstorm in Girrahween Park

*"To propose reality as a story rather than a story as reality
might at least remind you what a prior thing experience is."*
—Harold Brodkey

When the rain begins, I take shelter under an overhanging
rock ledge. I have often imagined that the Gadigal people
used this very cave and travelled along the same track,

musing and talking. The storm sweeps through the valley,
it possesses the trees and foliage, the rocks and ferns—
turbulent weather as spectacle—the wind whipping

the crowns of the trees in the middle distance
so the backs of their leaves appear silver in the rapidly
fading light, the thunder cracking and resounding

with enough force to terrify the neighbourhood dogs,
while the headlights on the opposite hill are gradually
obscured by rolling clouds, until I cannot see the hill

at all, more aware now of the noise the rain makes
as it hits the fallen leaves, the sandstone above my head,
the bush around me—a volume that I only fully appreciate

when I remove my earphones and halt *The New Yorker*
podcast of Harold Brodkey's "Dumbness is Everything".
The rain is fierce—water speeding down the sides

of the rock, dripping off the edge, collecting in a pool
in the elevated bed that I assumed would be a good place
to sleep if you were homeless, but which I now realise

is totally unsuited to the purpose I imagined. Just then,
a completely drenched woman appears on the track
below, and I call out to her. She looks up and grins

without pausing to consider my offer of refuge. Once
you are that wet, you might as well just keep on walking.
I have to be home soon to change and go out for dinner,

but as I'm dry and shielded from the teeming rain,
I'm not the least bit tempted by the prospect of stepping
out into the deluge. Brodkey's story of a couple fucking

on the lawn in a sea of moonlight fills my ears and I'm
as much in awe of the writing, which is ornate and arresting,
as I am in awe of the storm. There is a certain prescience

in what I am listening to—the animal dumbness of coupling
and Brodkey's insistence that he can't really take you there,
just as I cannot recreate the tumbling, frenetic rain,

which is now easing. Nor can I precisely convey the delight
of finding a whooshing, roaring tumult sounding ahead of me,
where a pop-up urban installation—Girrahween Falls—

must be crossed to leave the park. There is no other route
but to step gingerly onto the rocks submerged by rushing
water. I have no phone to capture the beauty and incongruity

of this apparition, just as I can't convey to Rhys, the local
bottle-shop proprietor, the unexpected pleasure of witnessing
the storm and the waterfall. A fire truck is blocking the road

and the electrical substation near the RSL has exploded.
An officer tells me that I cannot pass, that it's not safe.
¡No pasarán! I think briefly of the war to free Nicaragua,

then realising that I might not make it home at all, I ignore
the caution and run towards the lights glowing on the hill,
into another reality, another ending that I am yet to experience.

A Wall of Eyes

"Mengele was capable of being so kind to the children, to have them become fond of him, to bring them sugar, to think of small details in their daily lives."
—Auschwitz prisoner doctor

The woman in front of me died, her body held upright
by the people packed around her. Although it was winter

the truck was hot, the air rationed. When the doors
were finally flung open, we had no choice but to step

on the bodies of those who did not make it. Loud music
played from somewhere and a man wearing white gloves

walked up and down, whistling Wagner. I wondered
where I was, if I had arrived in heaven. He asked if

there were any twins on the train. Mother held us close
and whispered, say nothing. But someone must have

pointed us out. He took us away to a cosy dormitory.
I bagged the bunk bed above my brother's. He came

to see us that afternoon, wearing a white coat, but no gloves.
"Call me Uncle Pepi," he said. He gave us chocolate

and explained that if we did as he asked, we would
see our mother again soon. The next morning he led us

into his office. Opposite his desk—a whole wall of eyes.
Blue eyes, green eyes, grey eyes, speckled and shining

eyes—all staring at me. I fell down on the floor.
When I came to, my brother was holding a stethoscope

to my chest, listening to my heartbeat. Uncle was testing
a new medicine that would give us beautiful blue eyes.

It was almost ready. I had always been partial
to my brown eyes, but I said nothing. "Remove

your clothes," he said, "I'm collecting data."
The metal ruler was cold against my skin.

He wrote the numbers down with a fountain pen
like the one my father used to write his letters.

He took blood from my left arm, praising my bravery.
He took blood from my right arm. He took blood

from my brother, too. I wanted to ask if I
would get my blood back, but I was afraid.

He gave us sweets and said he would see us
presently. We had more to eat in Auschwitz,

but I missed my mother. I missed sprinting along
the cobblestones by the wall of the Łódź ghetto.

One night we were woken by these Russian soldiers
who spoke a strange language, rich as treacle. At first,

I did not understand. Later, gazing into a mirror,
I saw my brown eyes. I was lucky. I see that now.

After the Deluge

*"Every human war is now, automatically, a war against
the earth."*
—Robert Hass

Now, even more than before, we are shaped
by what we cannot see. Take Fatima, who was born
with a cleft palate, fused fingers and one missing leg.
The doctors held grave fears for her heart as well,
though she wasn't the worst they had seen. Sure,
there are explanations—depleted uranium,
with its astonishing ability to pierce armour and shatter
reinforced concrete, leaves a radioactive residue
that seeps into the soil, the water table. To say nothing
of the lead and mercury released by the bombs
dropped on Fallujah and now present in these
floating grains of dust just waiting to be inhaled.

Fatima propels herself along the path by the Euphrates
with the gait of a praying mantis, her crutches producing
a ravenous stride and a speed that is breathtaking.
She stops now and then to scold other children
and their irresponsible parents who are feeding
white bread to marbled ducks—ducks that were lucky
to survive the shock and awe unleashed upon them—
the poisons in the food chain, the shrinking wetlands,
their fertility as fragile as the tissue-thin eggs
lying in their nests. Apart from the rising and setting
of the sun, nothing is *automatic*. A drop of defiance
can become a ripple and then a river—take
the surgical separation of Fatima's fingers

so she can hold up, in front of her beaming face,
a V for victory; take the flapping outspread wings
and stuttering steps of a teal duck as it walks on water.

Shooting Footage

"Only that which narrates can make us understand."
—Susan Sontag

Let me introduce Joshua. I have decided
to begin with a close-up of his amber eyes
twinkling behind plastic lenses. His glasses
are quite thick and not at all flattering
for an eleven-year-old boy. A nerd. Joshua
quizzes me about apertures and anamorphosis,
his curiosity lighting up the room.

He has shiny black hair that tends
to kink up at the back of his neck.
His classmates pull his hair when they pass him
in the corridors. They call him greasy head
and oil can. They claim they have enough gunk
to lubricate the chains of their bicycles.
They wipe their hands on their trousers and laugh.

On the bus ride home, they use Joshua
for target practice. It is truly amazing
how far some boys can spit. Five boys own
the back seat, while another holds Joshua still
in the middle of the aisle. They dredge up
globules of sputum from deep in their throats
and propel them at Joshua. The sticky

white saliva contrasts starkly with his black hair.
Some of it clumps together like gruel,
some of it runs down and fouls
the collar of his white shirt. I film it
from the front of the bus, zooming in
on the visible pain on Joshua's face,
then the glee on the faces of the bullies.

I know from talking to Joshua that Fridays
at lunchtime are the worst. He won't tell me
what happens, he simply stares at his shoes.
So I arrange to meet my daughter's teacher
to discuss her spelling problems on a Friday,
just before lunchtime. I carry my camera
in my bag. Afterwards, I film my daughter

and her friends playing hopscotch. I wait
until I see the boys. They are dragging Joshua
towards the Disabled Toilet. It's so easy to shift
the viewfinder onto their procession. They carry him
like a trussed pig, stopping twice to yank
at his arms as if they hope to liberate them
from their sockets. My anger smoulders

like white-hot coals. I can barely contain it.
A boy punches Joshua in the stomach.
Another kicks him. They grab his shorts
and pull them down. Someone opens the door
and the steam rushes out. Joshua's glasses fog up
so he can't see. They push him inside, slamming

the door. "Let him eat bacon sandwiches,"
one of them says as they run off, laughing so much
that they're in danger of crying.
I film it all in one long take. It's the hardest
thing I've ever had to do, to film this and not
intervene. The Principal does not believe
that children can do this, that it happens at his school.

Yet I have this barbaric montage, these frames
of technicolour truth. And a silence I will end soon—
walls of brick and barbed wire, tumbling, tumbling down.

Beached Dreams

After Kenneth Slessor's "Beach Burial"

Silently and gladly to the reefs of Christmas Island
the convoys of asylum seekers come;
at night they cling to the boards of wooden boats that roll
and list in heaving seas.

Between the fob and mincing of the sound bite,
no one, it seems, has time for this—
to pluck them from a watery grave, wrap them in blankets
and raise a glass to honour

their remarkable courage, their very ordinary dreams
and their right to be proudly Australian. Instead,
we drive shards of broken tidewood into their beating hearts,
sealed by the signature

of our feckless leaders, written with such pragmatic
cowardice, with such unfeeling stubbornness
that the words choke as they begin—*"Unknown human"*—
the ink bleeds and fades

in a sea strewn with the wreckage of decency,
the withdrawal of compassion, the failure
of a nation to face its fear, to understand that, like all of us,
they come in the hope of a better life.

Nauru/Papua New Guinea

Three

You can tell a true war story
by the way it never seems to end.

Tim O'Brien, *How to Tell a True War Story*

All You Know

Crouching in the belly of the beast it smells bad—
gasoline fumes, sweat, the fear coming off
your skin. You've always been afraid of heights,
so it's some consolation to be strapped
to the metal ribcage of this raptor as it flies
over coconut groves and flooded rice paddies.
The Huey lands safely in a field beside a road—
deserted—and you head north-east, low hills
at your back, the sky a concrete grey pressing down.
A jumbled, wooden mess that was once a bridge
floats in the Sui Da Bang River, a squealing pig scurries
past a burnt-out hut, an old woman stares as you pass
and you are not sure if you're desired or despised.
An hour later, you wade through the knee-high
ferns of a rubber plantation, the trees spaced
out as symmetrically as marching soldiers.
Thumbs down, a warning shout and you dive
forward, rifle ready, just as the sky collapses
with monsoonal urgency, the water sluicing
over your hootchie in frantic streams—then
white light, thunder. Des appears and tells you
to recce up ahead and see if Charlie's out there.
Like the day you played football in a hailstorm,
you run with your forearm shielding your face,
but if the enemy's about, you cannot find them.
That's all you know. Soon darkness slides
over everyone and the word comes through

that Dave's been hit and hasn't made it.
The rain stops as suddenly as it started.
You are numb, scared, thirsty. You listen
to the night, to the staccato rhythm
of water dripping onto the red, sodden earth.

The Mathematics of War

At school, I tried to follow Butch's explanations
of calculus and trigonometry, but his penetrating stare
and the aura of his shining head and bristling eyebrows
often left me immobilised with fear, sheltering
behind my desk. I'd watched him punch boys
for not paying attention, for failing tests,
for uncompleted homework, I'd watched his sudden
right cross strike for reasons I did not understand.
Back then, I knew nothing about the mathematics of war—
how we would set up our ambushes in the shape of a triangle
with two machine guns at the points of the base,
in a line that ran parallel to the killing ground,
the third gun trained on the connecting track
so we covered the entrances and exits, and later
could calculate the probable and confirmed body count
as if they were merely numbers chalked on a blackboard.

As the sun sinks below the orderly rows of rubber trees
and the stars from distant galaxies glimmer,
I recall how Pythagoras discovered that the consonance
and dissonance floating out of a blacksmith's forge
depended on the weight ratio of the hammers striking
an anvil. He believed that the orbits of heavenly bodies
produced a celestial hum that we cannot hear,
but might describe with the right equation. Glancing
at the harmonious moon, I break open my M79,
load the shell and raise the leaf sight so I can focus
on a range of three hundred and seventy-five metres,
where the explosion will kill everyone who would fit

comfortably into a typical classroom. I wonder if I
could graph the projectile motion of the tracer bullets
that will soon fly from my Slaughtermatic at a rate
of seven hundred revs a minute, with a muzzle velocity
of eight hundred and fifty-three metres a second.

But the problem is too hard for my weary mind.
Instead, I wait for men and women dressed in black
to run into a zone whose existence is unknown to them.
Personally, I'd want more than a probable survival rate
of zero over zero, an indeterminate expression that depends
on the pressure I apply to the trigger. What if I don't act?
Will I slip over to the other side of the equation? Become
as cold and bloodless as a statistic? I am not a machine,
even though they've trained me to kill like one.
As Butch might have predicted, I've never excelled
at mathematics or war. What hope do I have
of finding a solution? I draw a line in the ground
with the tip of my index finger. Particles of red dirt
cling to my pink fingernail and in the silence
I sense the ethereal choirs of unborn children.

The Minimalist Kitchen

In Napoleon's day
     the army went
everywhere
     with its own cooks—
but I only have
     my stove—
a ration tin
     of Irish stew
I've punctured
     and refashioned
so it lets in air,
     but shields
the hexamine tablet
     from the wind.
I add curry powder
     to my sausages
floating in red goo
     and wait patiently
for my dinner
     to boil.

No brace
     of pheasants,
no hens
     laying eggs,
no suckling pig
     turning on the spit.
I remember
     my mother's steak
and kidney pie,

how the pastry
had the golden
        hue of a Phuoc Tuy
sunrise,
        how the mahogany table
was covered
        with white lace,
how you registered
        the weight of a knife,
a fork,
        as soon as you
picked one up.

This won't taste
        like a barbecued
sanga
        with its lovely
blackened skin,
        the thick-cut
caramelised onions,
        the freshly buttered
bread,
        but at least when
I eat
        most evenings,
what I lift to my lips
        is hot
and I'm not trying
        to kill

some poor bugger—
        though for all I know,
the poor buggers
        are about
to kill me.

The Firefight

You don't remember much
afterwards. You don't want to.
Though you dream it over
and over again—waking
under a sheet you've twisted
around your sweating body
as the sound of rapid fire
bludgeons the night & green
tracers fly about like some kind
of phosphorescent plague.
You hear a man scream obscenities
& another voice shout orders
with the same plosive panic
that has entered your bloodstream.
You feel the recoil dig
into your shoulder like shock,
glimpse the brilliant yellow flash—
a Catherine Wheel exploding
out of the grey palings of the back fence.
Des appears beside you, his thumb
hauling you in the direction of safety.
You hoist your pack & crabwalk
after him, before a monsoon
of mortar shells drops right there—
on the piece of dirt where you were
lying ... though in your dream
you are stricken, petrified, legless—
unable to run or crawl or do anything
to escape the barrage raining down
on you, night after sleepless night.

Searching the Dead

The bone-coloured branches of the rusty fig
twist and rise into a canopy of leaves that shuts
out the beating sun. It's like standing in a limestone cave
and gazing up at limbs that resemble toned calves
and bulging biceps. As if the tree has been fashioned
out of human body parts miraculously glued together.
From a distance it appears sublime, but standing beneath it,
I can't shift these images of haunches, thighs and elbows.
The human form, even when you're not looking for it,
is everywhere. Five days out from Nui Dat, after the firefight
and the ambush, I went back into the rubber plantation
to search the pockets of the dead. They weren't our dead,
our dead had been dusted off that morning, but here
were men who resembled us, soldiers who had been trained
to follow SOP, move carefully day and night, minimise risk.
Clothes now stretched tightly over bloated arms and legs,
feet cold and green, flies and gnats crowding around
their eyes, their mouths. Bodies washed clean by the rain,
a few with legs completely missing, one or two
without heads. We were searching for intelligence.
I found a gold American watch, sunglasses, a plastic comb,
a bag of uncooked rice, a lock of hair. Occasionally,
what appeared to be a diary, filled with Vietnamese script,
a pressed flower fluttering down to the ground.
A cowrie shell bringing the news from the South China Sea.
In one man's pockets a pair of lacy black knickers.
And photos wrapped in plastic to preserve them—
a girlfriend leaning against a motorbike, a couple posing

near a lake, a family in front of a shimmering pagoda.
Everything smeared with the same red dust that coated
my skin. There won't be another photograph of this man
sitting with his children as he tucks into a steaming soup.
The rubber trees had been hit by bullets and dribbled
latex, as if they were crying. Johnno and Boffa
were digging a mass grave. I took my shirt off
so I could feel the sun on my back. I might have been
fielding at square leg, dreaming of the tea break.
When I opened a tin of tiger balm or laid down a pack
of playing cards, this shiver spread from my neck
to my shoulders. I was so aware of my body, how
it was greased and primed, how it wasn't going to jam.
What I collected I put down by the base of the banyan tree,
the wood darker than this fig, soldiering on through
the hot afternoon, soaked with sweat. I was elated to be alive.
The work had to be done before we could move out.
I made a shrine to lives well lived, then went to find
some cool water to drink, some fresh air to breathe.

Jumping Jack Flash

A limp breeze from the north.
A waterbird lifts from the mangroves. I watch
until the glare of the sun makes me look away.
A stand of bamboo shifts in the heat haze.
Behind it, the village we will soon cordon and search.
Those dark frightened eyes staring at us.
We walk along this dry creek bed. Suddenly
I glimpse a white flash up ahead, hear
the boom and I know that someone has stepped
on a mine. His right leg, long strips of flesh
hanging off it, as if he's been flensed.
His left foot is not there, it's nowhere.
His left thigh grated, minced, covered in blood.
So much blood. It's Boffa—face white,
a hole above his belt the size of a football.
The effortless spawn of a jumping jack.
Johnno calls for Des to come quick,
but it's too late. There's nothing to do.
He's my friend and there's nothing
to do. I don't pick up my Slaughtermatic,
dash into the village and blaze away.
I feel nothing. I sit down on this
blasted land while they call for dustoff.
The flesh hanging off his legs in strips.

Under the Bed

After Boffa has been wrapped tight
in his hootchie and dusted off, we enter
this village whose name no one seems to know.
Yelling loudly, we move from house to house,
gathering the old, the women, the babies,
the children too young to fight, the men
who are not working in the fields.
We herd them into a makeshift holding pen
until they are pressed up against each other,
like cattle. Then we separate the men
of fighting age, as one might pick out
stones from a clay pot full of rice.

We make them squat with their legs open,
so our South Vietnamese interrogators
can kick and pummel their wedding tackle
until they give the required answers—
the location of tunnel entrances, the whereabouts
of Viet Cong leaders, the names of anyone
who feeds and harbours the enemy.

On a second sweep of the houses, I follow
Johnno into a room which holds a double bed
and not much else. He senses something, some
slight movement under the bed and he's firing
his submachine gun up and down the length
of the mattress, emptying the whole
cartridge, until the bed takes on the semblance

of a rattan screen and blood slowly
slides out and seeps down into the earth.

I can't really describe what concentrated fire
at close range does to a body—the mangled
faces, the sudden stink of lacerated organs,
the masses of blood, the horror, the horror …
When we pull them out from their hiding place
we discover that they are not armed—two men
about the same age as us, who were probably
just confused, frightened, hoping to stay alive.
Johnno looks at me and I respond with a nod
and we seal a contract to keep quiet and say
nothing. One after the other, we drag the men
by their ankles and lay them down
beside the drainage ditch that runs along the street.

What I see next I have no desire to remember,
but cannot easily forget—how one woman
screams, ducks under the white tape and runs
towards her husband? her lover?—until she is
stopped by a rifle butt crunching into her chest,
slips, falls and stays down in the dirt, crying.

I have no desire to remember how
she peers up at me, her pain burning
like an accusation laid out
before the whole village, before all of us—

men, women and children—who have watched this
and cannot do a thing to prevent or explain
or rescind what has just happened
and will never be mentioned in the official
dispatches to the generals and others
who are concerned with the conduct of the war.

The Book of Screams

Each day in hospital I wake
to a reading from *The Book of Screams.*
It comes, apparently, from the bathroom
situated two-thirds of the way along the hall.
No one talks while the screams linger.
I pass the time by counting in my head.
Thirty-five. Seventy-two. One hundred
and nine. Two hundred and thirty-one.
The screams are high-pitched and continuous,
as if she has been chosen for her ability
to hold the note, to produce abrasive chords
when her lungs must be almost airless and empty.
The ruckus shakes the thin partition around my bed,
it rattles the cups and saucers in the kitchen,
and threatens to shatter the high frosted panes
of glass that leach feeble light onto the floorboards.

At midday and again in the evening I reluctantly
listen to recitals from *The Book of Screams.*
Afterwards, the ward is sombre with silence.
By the third day, I cannot bear it any longer,
I leave my game of solitaire and march down
the corridor to see for myself, drawn to
the noise the way iron filings are attracted
to magnetic north. Two nurses cradle
a young girl, supine, in a bathtub.
Her eyes are closed, her lips collapse
into an involuntary O that corresponds
to the coordinates of her mouth. Her skin,
though I am not sure you can still call
it that, is the black of newly laid bitumen.

Impossible to comprehend agony—
to understand how one scream seems
to necessitate another, to grasp how a voice
can travel over rice paddies and rubber plantations,
under jungle canopies and down boulevards
resplendent with French architecture, before lifting
into the flying arches and buttresses of the mind,
until we are all dwelling in a cathedral of screams
whose substantial form cries out for mercy.

But I have no mercy to give. I gaze
in dumb horror at her right leg, where
the white ghost of her femur shines
through murky water, at the charred
oozing mess of a knee. Her body is
no more than a diaphanous veil hanging
between this world and the next.

Later, they tell me about the morning
of the bombing and its aftermath.
Now, when I hear the word *napalm,*
I remember that girl's face,
her eyes opening as I turn
to leave, her raw cries staying
with me and spiralling outwards,
forever travelling, like radio waves
rolling end over end
into the windless chasms of space.

Rock the Baby

Talking doesn't make it any better,
despite what the shrinks say—the words
remain locked in my head as if
I'm a pinball machine stuck on TILT
with the lights flashing and the alarm sounding
as one steel ball after another is sucked
down into oblivion. But let me tell you
about Johnno—an athlete, a natural soldier,
a top bloke. Johnno was a talker.
He talked to anyone and everyone,
especially the street kids. He was always
buying them ice creams and giving them yoyos.
How he came by so many yoyos, I don't know,
must have bought the lot from hawkers, I guess.
I can still see Johnno surrounded by kids
as he demonstrates how to walk the dog,
how to go around the world and his party trick—
rock the baby in the cradle. Johnno
could do anything with a yoyo. Anything.

We're on patrol, nine days out of Nui Dat,
near the hamlets south of Binh Ba,
when Johnno says he's sick of humping
Claudia, the radio he carries. Will I babysit her?
I agree. He spies this kid in shorts
and saunters towards him with his yoyo flying
over his shoulder on one continuous loop.
I sit in the scrappy shade of a rubber tree,

and watch this boy reach up
and grab the pocket of his fatigues
and lead Johnno into the village.

We found him later, face-down
between two huts, and yeah,
he was gone round the bloody world
alright, he was in some kind of perpetual
orbit, lying there in that red dirt
with a neat hole in his head, the string
of the yoyo unfurled beside him.
He trusted the kid. He was so naive,
like he almost expected them to walk up
and say, by the way, you do realise
we're all Viet Cong here?
I've still got that yoyo. That's why
I never talk about the fucking war,
because, you know, what is there to say?

Back Home

I walked into the newsagent's
where I'd had a paper round
before school, tossing the daily
onto porches while I cycled past
with no hands. Old man Doyle
took one look at me and said,
"How many yellow bastards
did you kill, son?"

I stared at him, put my
five cents down on the counter,
picked up a newspaper
then turned and walked away.
How could he ask me that?
And how was I meant to answer?

Four

I saw the angel in the marble
and carved until I set him free.

Michelangelo

Housing the Mind

If you could afford an architect and a master builder,
what would you construct to house the mind?
Would you wall it in snugly, or request cathedral vaults
so your thoughts might soar through the octaves
in arias that celebrate, not success, but the simple
act of striving, as Einstein did, searching
for a unified field theory that was always just
out of reach, that he'd put down somewhere,
in some room, though for the life of him
he couldn't remember where? Would you go for
the open-plan ambience of a warehouse conversion,
or a house on stilts, level with the canopy, windows
opening to birdsong, to bushfire winds scouring
the valley, to a pair of tawny frogmouths nesting
in a blue gum, a discovery accompanied
by the puzzling arrival of a dappled feather in the mail?

No, perhaps you'd take your brief from childhood—
the room beyond the house, the granny flat,
where you slept each night with your brother,
listening to possums scampering across the roof,
dropping ideas like acorns, like all the notions
about yourself you've been forced to shed, the gap
between what you have to offer and the doors slamming
shut in front of your face with the predictability
of Maxwell Smart walking the long tunnel, then hesitating
as the swinging steel catches the tip of his nose.

Some would probably hanker for a library,
a reading room of medieval design with precious
books stacked low to high, or perhaps with redwood shelves
lining a domed ceiling that can only be reached
by a ladder, the workspace flowing along the wall
beneath the windows, its length giving both a sense
of sprawl and the suggestion of a track
winding through the bush, without signposts,
but still easy enough to follow. Others would
no doubt want a kitchen—the ladles, utensils
and pans hanging above the island bench,
the expanse of gas jets reminiscent of Neolithic
stone circles, the scent of cardamoms, cloves
and crushed garlic a prelude to abundance.

I'd definitely choose a cluttered studio—canvases
stacked everywhere, the hogshair brushes upright
in a biscuit tin, the teapot, the squat Kelvinator
near the sink, a green armchair with wonky springs,
postcards pinned to the noticeboard with the overlapping
confusion of a découpage tray, along with an array
of places you could park the easel, depending
on your mood and the light streaming through
the oversized window that the carpenter installed
as an afterthought, when an especially large canvas
wouldn't fit through the door. A good story
to tell with a smoky single malt in your hand.

The Study Before the Major Work

I have learnt from experience that you must begin
with the white page in your sketchbook, the canvas
on your easel, your gaze fixed to the world
that assembles you with improbable grace.
Today, I pick up a piece of charcoal and sketch the barista
who stands behind the machine he calls "Generalissimo".
Lava flows from the chrome spouts, steam rises.
His eyebrows are deadly! A face to launch a thousand
crushes. There's so much you can achieve with a single line.
I stare at the stubble that lies fallow on his cheek, follow
the way he eases the milk jug into the pressurised air
as if he is handling a jittery horse. The regulars wait
for their fix with a barely contained Pavlovian patience.
A man reads a newspaper as if nothing else exists,
a woman clutches a phone to her ear like a singer
striving for harmony, an elderly lady orders
hot chocolate in a bowl and takes as much pleasure
in warming her hands as she does in drinking.
I finish one sketch and start another, in love
with the repetition that is the texture of my life,
waking each morning to currawong calls,
raising the blinds to the shifting architecture
of light, dressing in loose clothes, keen to dwell
in the lilting halls of wonder. I draw as he fills cup
after cup, until he carries a latte and macchiato
to the high stools by the window. His thumb
grazes his sideburn, my blackened fingers curl
around the tall glass. At last the café is quiet.
We sip without speaking, for what is there to say?
The caffeine skids through my heart like sudden rain.

Ash Wednesday, Aireys Inlet

When the wind turned and the fire surfed
the hills, the whole town gathered on the beach.
We stood with our backs to the sea, gazing
at the firestorm which seemed to occupy
both the present and the future. Home after home
will soon be wiped out by a tsunami of heat,
an incendiary argument that scoffs at human wishes,
at any notion of what might be fair or just,
that treats the beautiful and the ugly
with the same scorching malevolence. It's quite
a show—outlandish pomp and pathos
as the flames swing, tumble and twist—acrobats
in a darkened big top. This fire is a circus clown
without a sense of humour, but what strikes me
most about the scene is how it subverts
our customary ways of seeing. So many paintings
feature the magnanimous sky as if it holds
an answer to questions we struggle to articulate.
In the foreground, people are clumped upright,
brushes in a jar, while fury rages above them
like the medieval idea of hell, like the molten slag pool
in movies that has become the only way to destroy
the One Ring, the Terminator, the Alien. When I paint
the burning trees, I find solace in the knowledge
that the bush is reborn through fire. But what of us?
Beside me in the shallow water, people dodge the falling
embers. All I can do is capture the pain on their faces,
how they long to turn away, but watch transfixed.

The Swimmer

After Jan Senbergs

It comes from an unknown place, this mystery,
and I let it come, my hand raised, colours mixed,
my brush intent on singing. Tonight, I sense
the whole painting before I begin—the gullies
and gutters of the endless sea, the dark waves
lifting along ridge lines, the way the distant
peaks look like snow-capped mountains
and the white foam mimics the mane
of a brindled mare bolting across the windswept tundra.

A man swims in the heaving sea. His arm leaves the water
and cuts through the icy air, his head rotates, his fingers
are splayed as they break the surface, then disappear.
There is no land in sight, the water is very cold
and no one on the boat, it seems, has spotted the swimmer.
It is merely an act of imagination, you are thinking
and you may be right, but still he is swimming—
arms fierce in their rhythm, feet kicking against
the current, shoulders rising and falling with the swell,
his skin slowly taking on the blue hue of the sea.

Meaning rises from the literal just as salt spray is flung up
from the lip of a wave. You might laugh at my hopeless
hope, this fascination I have with how we live through images.
Or you might grasp the purity of this moment—
when he opens his blessed mouth to breathe.

Flannel Flowers

After Cressida Campbell

So we haven't had sex for three months—
should I be worried? My friend's husband
went overseas when she was ill, without her.

Unpacking his suitcase on his return,
she lifted up his favourite coral sweater
and these crimson packages fell out, sailing

down to the floor like autumn leaves. At first
she thought they were the chocolate hearts
that restaurants give you. But looking closer,

she realised that the packages were condoms.
The background is the blue of optimism—
that sensation you get when you lie on the grass

and stare into a summer sky until your mind floats
where it will, without objective or obligation.
Backgrounds are always with us, as ordinary

and as extraordinary as birth and death.
I carve the flannel flowers into the woodblock
with a *Hangi To* and the knife cleaves

to my thumb and forefinger. The petals
flare in the cool breeze—some drooping,
some twisting back on their stems, some still

closed, their green tips rising like madrigals.
There are no useful models for how a relationship
endures—at least none that make sense to me.

What I remember of my parents was the absence
of a cross voice in the house and the weary resignation
of my mother listening to my father tell some stranger

that the first sixty-four years of marriage
are the worst. I have no room for improvement,
no desire to know everything about you. Just

as I ease my way into this block—slowly,
slowly—each carved line a gesture I refuse
to explain, how I long to feel your fingers press

into my back, the flannel flowers somersaulting
in riotous joy, the blue sky lifting & lifting, our
breath escaping in gasps—wordless and resinous.

Doubt and Constant Rain

Perched on the balcony rail, sheltering from the rain,
the magpie's chest puffs out—an impasto drag queen.
Her topaz eyes peer at me with the sort of quizzical

intensity that demands answers, but all I can do
is think how the sharp, dusky point of her beak
is like the first mark I make on canvas when I know

and do not know what I want to paint. Walking
along the bush path near home, having saluted
the swamp mahogany which rises next to the track

like some old crone who has seen everything, I spy
two beagles ahead of me—poised, uncertain—puzzling
over whether I am friend or foe. I pause to calculate

the size and capacity of their teeth before I edge
towards them. It takes just one wag of the tail
and they leap into delirious motion, satisfied

that my appearance warrants a frolic around my feet.
It's quite familiar, the process that slows time right down
until you hold fear in your fingertips, while an insistent

voice inside your head says, Come off it! You call
yourself an artist? Please! Who painted *this*?
I prefer to laugh at myself with the dangling

wet tongue and floppy ears of a boisterous beagle
out and about on a fragrant afternoon, while I
move these black globules around my palette,

remembering how Cézanne painted the same dish
of apples over and over again, as I confront
this curious bird before she flees into the falling rain.

Degas's Women

There are so many
of us and we are beautiful.
You probably notice our skin first,
how the pores glisten with the patina
of eternity. Some critics have called
our poses ungainly, while others
have praised the naturalism of a leg
extended over the rim of an iron
bath, the fierceness of a brush
combing hennaed hair, the modest
toil of a towel in motion.

We are Degas's nudes
and we are washing. There is no
shame in that, though there are
some who find the body shameful,
who want to shroud us in funereal
black, constrain the dangers
of the domestic sublime.

We are rarely identified,
seldom named. A mole beckons
from under a shoulder-blade
in one pastel, the deep crease
of a backbone in another.
Antoinette, Despina, Clarice—
do you think you know us?
Perhaps you have imagined
how you would arrange a limb

or pour water from a jug, but
the fantasy and how it plays out
in reality are never close.

　　　We have turned away
so you may never glimpse
our faces, cannot know our thoughts,
can only observe how we sink
into the welcoming warmth
and let the day's demands
and other people's cruel words
fall from our shoulders
with an endless sigh.

　　　When you look again,
nothing will have changed—
that is the mundane truth
that Degas understood—how
the steam rises from the antique
dome of a knee like steam.

Drawing: the essentials

So long to conceptual art,
where the idea is a gilded thought
dissolving into vacancy and loss,
while beyond the gutter party—
this festering sinkhole of stubbies,
plastic bags & complacency,
the snagged fretwork of an umbrella,
the putrid odour of wasted talent,
gnats circling like winged acolytes.

So long to the novel of ideas
where the characters too neatly represent
the battle between knowledge and more
knowledge, where the obsessions
of the author lead into an arid desert
that bakes and annuls the soul
as a bare remnant of feeling slides
down the prickly incline of a cactus.
The cliques sleep in the sun like lizards.

Ignore them. Remember the taste of grappa
tossed back under a blossoming moon,
how the gaping mouth in the triptych
evokes the beauty of a Monet landscape.
My arm is extended, the oil stick
greases my hand. No mistakes, no
point beginning again—I will draw
with spontaneous intensity until I make
my final mark on the lidless world.

Barangaroo Capriccio

The sandstone blocks are large and rough-hewn,
as if they have been lifted from some ancient ruin
and arranged in terraces descending to the sea.
Everywhere there are signs. *No Swimming*
features a sketch of a shark swallowing
the wriggling legs of someone in spandex speedos
who resembles a former Prime Minister. Cue *Jaws*
soundtrack on an endless loop. The planet spins
at a speed that dazzles and for a moment I feel
as if I am stuck on that roller-coaster road
through the Eastern Suburbs, the girls in the car
behind me sporting sunglasses and Fair Isle sweaters
and screaming so loudly my insides rise up
in wordless agony. Desperate, I take the third exit
at the roundabout without losing them. The harbour
flows all night, ignoring maps, any notion of a king tide
as unfashionable as a Namatjira ghost gum, the colour
leaching into a cobalt sky. Coke bottles and plastic bags
sail down the streets of Cremorne Point, water laps
against the leadlight windows of an art deco apartment,
while a hazard beacon on the top of Harry Seidler's
Blues Point Tower flashes like a harbour-buoy, each
to each, and the cockatoos squawk above floating
Toyotas like soprano prophets high on helium.
O Atlantis. O Packer and Gomorrah. Nero was not
the only one who fiddled while Rome burned.
When I paint the drowned city, the lit offices sparkle
in an indigo sea—a flotilla of impotent, dying stars.

The Tomb of the Unknown Artist

After Grayson Perry

Denim, leather, tinsel, ceramic buttons, polypropylene,
polyurethane, glass, Norfolk pine, nails, glue, rope, silk, taffeta,
diamante beads, Swarovski crystals, paper, human carcass.

When the time finally comes, lay me out
in my painting smock and dungarees,
lace up my Blundstone boots, put
ceramic buttons over my eyes and weave
Christmas tinsel (silver and gold) through my hair.
Pack an esky of provisions—goat masala,
black pudding on sourdough toast for breakfast,
a bottle of sparkling shiraz to wash
it all down. I might not eat during this, my last
journey, but at least I won't have to ring
for takeaway when I arrive

on the other side. Drive this battered sloop
down to Clovelly and carry it over the concrete
sandbars. Tell anyone who happens to be passing
that I selected the tree by the rake of its trunk,
cut the stern plank with my own hands, planed
and shaped the timbers and stitched the sails
from op-shop evening dresses. Gorgeous work,
they'll say, as you lay me out over the thwarts
of the boat and lower it down into the sea.

Take an armful of my exhibition catalogues,
the ones that never attracted a single red dot,
and pile them up in the bow. Strike a match.
When the pyre ignites, push the vessel out
into the currents. As the cormorants bob
on the waves and the silver gulls swoop,
say whatever you couldn't say to my face,
then get on with your own good lives.
Film the whole jaunty wake and offer it
to gallery directors around the country—
the blazing farewell of an unknown artist.

Acknowledgements

A number of these poems have appeared in the following journals, newspapers and anthologies, some in earlier versions: *Australian Poetry Journal, Canberra Times, Communion Arts Journal, Cordite Poetry Review, fourW New Writing, Island, Mascara Literary Review, Stilts Journal, Weekend Australian Review; All These Presences* (ed. Jean Kent, David Musgrave and Carolyn Rickett, Puncher & Wattmann, 2016); *Buying Online* (Newcastle Poetry Prize Anthology, Hunter Writers Centre, 2018); *Grieve: Stories and Poems about Grief and Loss* (Vol 3, 2015 and Vol 5, 2017) both published by Hunter Writers Centre; *Joy: 2017 ACU Prize for Poetry* (Australian Catholic University, 2017); *Loving Kindness: 2016 ACU Prize for Poetry* (Australian Catholic University, 2016); *On First Looking* (ed. Jean Kent, David Musgrave and Carolyn Rickett, Puncher & Wattmann, 2018); *Peace, Tolerance & Understanding: 2015 ACU Prize for Poetry* (Australian Catholic University, 2015); *The Best Australian Poems 2015* (ed. Geoff Page) and *2016* (ed. Sarah Holland-Batt) both published by Black Inc.; *The Intimacy of Strangers* (ed. Andy Kissane and Philip Porter, Pret a Porter Publishing, 2018); *Writing to the Wire* (ed. Dan Disney and Kit Kelen, UWA Publishing, 2016). I would like to express my gratitude to the editors of these publications.

"Alone Again" won the *Australian Poetry Journal*'s 2015 Poem of the Year.

"After the Deluge" and "Ash Wednesday, Aireys Inlet" were highly commended in the 2015 Tom Collins Poetry Prize.

"Rock the Baby" won the 2017 Tom Collins Poetry Prize.

"All You Know", "The Mathematics of War", "The Firefight", "Jumping Jack Flash" and "Under the Bed" were shortlisted in the 2018 Newcastle Poetry Prize.

"Marriage Material" was commissioned for *Marriage Material: a 1903 Wedding*, a Marrickville Library exhibition featuring Margaret Meek's wedding dress.

"Beached Dreams" was published in the exhibition catalogue, *The Invisible* (UTS Gallery), and on the website, The Empathy Poems (www.empathypoems.com.au).

"Flannel Flowers" in response to *Flannel flowers* by Cressida Campbell, 2013, woodblock print, 98.7 x 155.8 cm, Philip Bacon Galleries, Brisbane.

"The Swimmer" in response to *The swimmer* by Jan Senbergs, 1994, synthetic polymer paint on canvas, 198.0 x 259.0 cm, Niagara Galleries, Melbourne.

"The Tomb of the Unknown Artist" in response to *The Tomb of the Unknown Craftsman* by Grayson Perry, 2011, cast iron, oil paint, glass, rope, wood, flint hand axe, 305 x 204 x 79 cm. British Museum, London.

My thanks to the Literature Board of the Australia Council for the Arts for a new work grant which supported the writing of this book. I'd like to thank the Booranga Writers' Centre for a residency that was made particularly enjoyable by the warmth of the Wagga Wagga community, especially David Gilbey. Thanks to Tim Langford for his superb cover, to Christine Bruderlin for her elegant design, and to my publisher, David Musgrave, for his ongoing support. I'd especially like to thank Judy Beveridge, Brook Emery, Susan Fealy, Martin Langford, David Musgrave and Alex Skovron for their comments on these poems.

Andy Kissane has published a novel, a book of short stories, *The Swarm*, and four books of poetry. Awards for his poetry include the Fish International Poetry Prize, the *Australian Poetry Journal*'s Poem of the Year, the Booranga Prize for Poetry, the Coriole National Wine Poet Prize and the Tom Collins Poetry Prize. *Radiance* was shortlisted for the Victorian and Western Australian Premier's Prizes for Poetry and the Adelaide Festival Awards. He recently co-edited a book of criticism on Australian poetry, *Feeding the Ghost*. He teaches Creative Writing and English in schools and universities. He lives in Sydney.

www.ingramcontent.com/pod-product-compliance
Lightning Source LLC
Chambersburg PA
CBHW031001090426
42737CB00008B/627